PUT OUT INTO THE
DEEP

PRAISE
FOR
PUT OUT INTO THE DEEP

One of the most important contributions of the Second Vatican Council was the renewed emphasis on the indispensable apostolate of the laity in the world. Sadly, it's also one of the most forgotten or misunderstood teachings. Stephen Gabriel's book brings great clarity and urgency to that teaching. His approach draws on the wisdom of the Church and addresses the needs of the present moment. This important work guides the laity first to the importance of their own formation, then through the spiritual dimension of evangelization, and finally to the work of the lay apostolate in various sectors of society. I recommend this book to the lay faithful as an excellent instrument for learning to live their proper vocation as leaven in the world.

—**Most Rev. Michael F. Burbidge, Bishop of Arlington, Virginia**

One of the things I appreciate most about this book is its emphasis on the importance of prayer and the sacraments in the life of the apostle. As Gabriel reminds us, we cannot do anything without the grace of God, and so we must constantly seek to deepen our union with Christ through prayer, the Eucharist, and the other sacraments. Whether you are a new Catholic just beginning to explore your faith or a seasoned veteran looking for fresh insights, this book is a must-read. So dive in, my friends, and discover the apostle you are called to be!

—**Fr. Rocky Hoffman, Chairman and CEO, Relevant Radio**

This is a book every lay person needs to read and every priest should be handing out! Building on the wisdom of the Saints and Popes, and filled with anecdotes from ordinary Catholics—the saints in our midst— Stephen Gabriel has taken seriously the Christian apostolic calling. This book shows how it can be done, without leaving your family or your job. I highly recommend this book to be read as widely as possible.

—**Jeffrey Morrow, Professor of Theology, Seton Hall University, Immaculate Conception Seminary School of Theology and Senior Fellow of the St. Paul Center for Biblical Theology**

Gabriel grounds the sharing of the Faith in loving and deep friendship with others in our family, parish, workplace, and social life. Even our suffering can be an occasion of helping others to get to know God. The anecdotes of his book brought tears to my eyes. No one, no one at all, is beyond the power of God's love which we can share in friendship.

—**Christopher Kaczor, Chair of the Department of Philosophy, Loyola Marymount University and Fellow in Bishop Barron's Word on Fire Institute.**

This short, punchy book covers a lot of ground. It is a rousing call to engage in the evangelizing mission of the Church addressed especially, in Stephen Gabriel's words, to her "advance troops"… that is, to the lay faithful. It offers concrete suggestions for a lifestyle primed for a generous apostolate, and suggests practical tips for doing so in the family, parish, workplace, and among friends. Among its best qualities are numerous, real-world anecdotes that make the material really hit home. This is a readable, no-nonsense book that doesn't shy away from the hard issues confronting modern apostles. Great for novices and veterans alike!

—**Fr. Carter Griffin, Rector, Saint John Paul II Seminary, Washington, DC**

The Lord Jesus' valedictory instruction to "go … and proclaim the Gospel to every creature" was given to every disciple, without expiration date. Yet many of his followers struggle to live the missionary dimension of our faith. Like his diaconal and archangelic namesakes, Stephen Gabriel shows all of us in this very accessible book how to propose the Good News attractively, courageously and effectively to family members, friends, coworkers, fellow parishioners, social media followers and all those Jesus will send to us. It's an excellent training manual for the modern apostle.

—**Fr. Roger J. Landry, Catholic Chaplain, Columbia University**

In the spirit of the first Christians, this book is an excellent guide for any Catholic who wants to become an apostle in spreading the Gospel and our faith in all circumstances of our daily lives. The inspiring personal stories of evangelization you will find in this book demonstrate the power of the Holy Spirit, who magnifies our limited efforts to bring our friends and everyone closer to Jesus Christ.

—**Fr. Charles Trullols, Director, Catholic Information Center, Washington, DC**

Our Father set up the world so that there are hundreds of millions more laymen than ordained. This means the primary responsibility for evangelizing the world is meant for us. In his powerful new book, layman Stephen Gabriel explains how the world is ours and everyone in it, and therefore we must get busy with the personal apostolate. His book will inspire you to ask those questions that may seem frightening to ask: "Have you ever thought of becoming Catholic?" or, "Would you like to go to Mass with me?" or, "Have you been to confession lately?" Gabriel knows such questions will change lives and souls.

—**Austin Ruse, author of** *Under Siege: No Finer Time to be a Faithful Catholic*

Via inspiring and beautifully told personal stories, this book reminds all Christians how to best serve our fellows on this earth: evangelization. It's a perfect gift for graduates, newlyweds, parents, and grandparents—in fact, for any Catholic, at any stage of life.

—**Mary Eberstadt, author of** *Adam and Eve after the Pill* **and** *Adam and Eve after the Pill, Revisited*

Stephen Gabriel prays that he take the universal call to holiness seriously, and wants to help you to, as well. This book is a tremendously practical encouragement to be who God wants you to be by virtue of your Baptism. You can be His light. You can be His instrument. You can, by His grace, love like Him.

Take and read Put Out into the Deep *and please do share it with love, as you share God's love.*

—**Kathryn Jean Lopez, senior editor, National Review Institute and author of** *A Year With the Mystics: Visionary Wisdom for Daily Living*

PUT OUT INTO THE DEEP

BECOME THE APOSTLE YOU ARE CALLED TO BE

STEPHEN GABRIEL

Scepter

Put Out Into the Deep
by Stephen Gabriel

The total or partial reproduction of this book is not permitted, nor its informatic treatment, or the transmission by any forms or by any means, either electronic, mechanical, by photocopy or other methods, without the prior written consent of the copyright owners.

Unless otherwise noted, Scripture texts from the New and Old Testament are taken from the Holy Bible, Revised Standard Version Catholic Edition © 1965 and 1966 by the Division of Christian Education of the National Council of the Churches of Christ in the United States. All rights reserved.
All copyrighted material is used by permission of the copyright owner. No part of it may be reproduced without permission.

Published by Scepter Publishers, Inc., copyright © 2023
info@scepterpublishers.org
www.scepterpublishers.org
800-322-8773
New York

All rights reserved.

Cover Image: Raphael's The Miraculous Draft of Fishes
(ca. 1515–1516). Public Domain.
Cover Design: Studio Red Design
Page Design: Studio Red Design

Library of Congress Control Number: 2023904620
ISBN paperback: 9781594174902
ISBN eBook: 9781594174919

Printed in the United States of America

Table of Contents

Preface 1

Introduction 5

The Gospel Message and the Call to Evangelize........................9

The Church Calls on the Laity to Form the Front Lines of the Church's Life..13

Striving for Holiness 17

Growth in Our Knowledge of the Faith....................................19

First Prayer and Mortification—Then Action 21

The Witness of Everyday Christian Living 25

Apostolate in the Family Setting...27
    Family-Related Apostolic Stories 31

Apostolate in the Parish 41
    Parish-Related Apostolic Stories 44

Apostolate in the Workplace 49
    Workplace-Related Apostolic Stories 53

Apostolate in the Social Sphere...67
    Social-Related Apostolic Stories 69

The Apostolate of Suffering 85

The Apostolate of Public Opinion 87

Conclusion 91

Prayer for the New Evangelization 93

Preface

Why a book on apostolate? In particular, why a book on apostolate aimed at the laity? Because we, the laity, are called to spread the gospel message by Our Lord and Savior, Jesus Christ himself. As Christians, we have a duty to evangelize. Despite our call to be apostolic, however, most of us find it very difficult. Of course, we want what is best for those we care about, but sometimes we are more focused on their worldly needs and not concerned enough about their eternity. Sometimes, too, we haven't reflected deeply enough about how being a Catholic has changed us for the better. On top of that, some of us may be a little afraid of how others will respond. Will they think I'm a religious fanatic or some kind of holy roller? All of these reasons and others can incline us not to reach out to our friends and help them grow closer to Our Lord.

Fortunately, there's a solution for this condition: holiness! Despite our sins and defects, we are all called to be saints. But first, we need to want to be saints. We have to want to love Our Lord with all our being. Then, with some help, we can move in that direction. This book will address the need for personal holiness and the kind of love that leads to friendship, which is the foundation of our apostolate.

We also need a good knowledge of the Faith. We can't give what we don't have. So, we'll discuss the need for solid religious formation.

I think it's helpful to rid ourselves of the idea that we "do apostolate," as if we put on our apostolate hat in some circumstances and take it off in others. Rather, we should think of ourselves as apostles. We are apostles all the time—at home, at work, on the subway, walking the dog in the neighborhood, volunteering at the parish. Through our cheerful disposition and interest in others, we try to expand our circle of friendships and in doing so create the basis for digging deeper with some of our friends, learning what makes them tick, and sharing with them what makes us tick. These friendships provide the grist for our apostolate because we can help many of these friends grow closer to God in one way or another.

It's important to keep in mind that we're not trying to sell snake oil to the friends we are trying to bring closer to Our Lord. We love them and we want what is best for them. Some will be receptive and some won't. Nevertheless, if we are motivated by love, our friends will likely see that and appreciate our concern. We also need to remember that we are just poor instruments. This is the work of the Holy Spirit, and we are simply being asked to help give grace a chance. Thus, we put it all in God's hands, plant the seed, and pray for the fruit to emerge. It may not happen right away—it may take years. We do our best, we pray, and the rest is in God's hands.

This book discusses the various settings in which we can exercise our apostolate—home, work, parish, and community. There is no cookie-cutter way to evangelize. But we'll discuss each of these settings and how one might go about reaching out to those we encounter with the goal, of course, of developing friendships.

Each apostolic setting is followed by some real-life apostolic anecdotes. These are true stories of regular people (with fictitious names) who have made a difference in the life of a friend, colleague, or family member. Because of their love and concern they reached out and, in one way or another, helped someone grow closer to God. These stories are meant to inspire you to do something similar when the opportunities arise. Keep in mind that these people are not "apostolic dynamos." They are ordinary folks just like you and me. They are all sinners struggling to overcome their defects just like you and me. But their love for Our Lord and their love for their friends moved them to take a risk and make a difference—some in relatively small matters like arriving at daily Mass on time and some in very serious matters like converting to the Catholic faith.

Introduction

When I was in graduate school many years ago, recently married and recently resuming the practice of my Catholic faith, I was involved in a conversation about religion with a couple other graduate students. I believe we may have invited them over to our apartment in married student housing for wine and cheese some Saturday evening. At one point in the conversation one of our guests said something like, "If you really believe what Christians profess to believe, you should be evangelizing everyone you know." Frankly, I had never really thought much about that. I remember responding with something like, "That's what priests and nuns are for. It's their job to evangelize. They're the pros." Many years later, remembering that conversation and my response, it occurred to me that it's a good thing the early Christians didn't have my attitude. If they had, it's likely that Christianity never would have gotten off the ground. Thankfully, the early Christians were "on fire" with love for Our Lord and with love for their family and friends. They couldn't help but share the Good News with anyone who would listen.

The early Christians were eager to spread the gospel message because it changed their lives. Jesus Christ, his teachings, and his redemptive passion, death, and resurrection, changed everything and gave their lives purpose and meaning. And no doubt they took to heart Jesus' commandment "that you love one another; even as I have loved you, that you also love one another. By this all men will know that you are my disciples, if you have love for one another" (Jn 13:34–35). There are many factors that explain the spread of Christianity throughout the world. But the fundamental driving force was love—love for Our Lord and love for others.

So, we modern Christians have to ask ourselves, "How am I different from the early Christians?" For most of us, we can practice our faith without fear of persecution, unlike the early Christians. Most of us have had to experience a religious conversion of some kind. Even cradle Catholics have had to cross that threshold from practicing the faith of our parents to making the Faith our own. The conversion may have been very subtle, without our even noticing that it happened, but at some point we embraced the Catholic faith as our own.

Why don't we modern Catholics have that apostolic fervor of the early Christians? Maybe it's because, for many of us, our conversion was very subtle. We were not knocked off our horse like Saul of Tarsus. Maybe it's because we take for granted the incredible grace and blessings we've received. We aren't awestruck by the miracle of the Eucharist and the profound mystery of the Holy Mass. We don't fully appreciate the encounter we have with Jesus in the sacrament of penance when the weight of our sins is removed from our shoulders. Maybe we haven't reflected deeply enough or often enough on the incredible love that God, our Savior, has given us as evidenced by his becoming man and suffering an agonizing death for us on the cross so we can spend eternity with him in heaven. For many of us—though certainly not all—being a Catholic has been too easy. We don't appreciate what we have. The Faith has not changed us.

If we consider the wonderful treasure that we possess as Catholics, make the effort to learn more about our faith, and strive, through a life of prayer, to grow closer to Jesus, our Savior, we will indeed change. And our life will take on new meaning and, motivated by love, we too will want to share the Good News with others.

The Gospel Message and the Call to Evangelize

As Christians, we are followers of Christ. We are his disciples. This is what being Christian means. The Gospels make it very clear that Jesus called his followers to evangelize. Most of this book will discuss what this means in practical terms. It will be worthwhile, however, to consider Jesus' words, that is, his call to us to spread the Good News. Jesus sent seventy disciples to the surrounding towns and villages to prepare them for his arrival (Lk 10:1). Clearly, Jesus wants to involve his followers in the conversion of the world. There is no "maybe" about this. Jesus wants you and me engaged in the evangelization of our society.

"Then he said to his disciples, 'The harvest is plentiful, but the laborers are few; pray therefore the Lord of the harvest to send out laborers into his harvest'" (Mt 9:37–38).

Jesus, of course, is speaking of the harvest of souls. There was a great need during those days for disciples to reach out and interact with the many souls who had not heard the message of Jesus. And the need today is also great. We need only take a look around us at all the lost souls who are confused about so many things. Materialism and consumerism have become the new religion. Human sexuality has become distorted and errors are being promoted at the highest levels of government and society. There are many people who just need to talk with someone who has understanding and empathy and who can help them see the truth of who we are as children of God, destined for so much more than this world has to offer. Most of these people will not be reached by priests and nuns. They are your friends, neighbors, and colleagues. You rub shoulders with them every day. If you don't help them, who will?

> You are the light of the world. A city set on a hill cannot be hid. Nor do men light a lamp and put it under a bushel, but on a stand, and it gives light to all in the house. Let your light so shine before men, that they may see your good works and give glory to your Father who is in heaven. (Mt 5:14–16)

Jesus referred to his disciples as the "light of the world." And so we are. We are light not due to anything we've accomplished. The light that we radiate comes from Jesus himself. If we embrace his teaching, cooperate with his grace, struggle to overcome our defects and weaknesses, and love those Our Lord has placed in our path, the light of Christ will shine forth wherever we go. The alternative is to place our light under a bushel basket. We should keep in mind that we will all have to answer to God for how we respond to the incredible grace and blessings we've been given. Better that we follow Our Lord's command to "let your light so shine before men."

Jesus made it clear that his Church's mission is to bring souls to him. After the miraculous catch of fish, he told Peter, "Do not be afraid; henceforth you will be catching men" (Lk 5:10). As disciples of Christ and members of his Church, that is our mission too.

The Church Calls on the Laity to Form the Front Lines of the Church's Life

Pope St. John Paul II quotes Pius XII in calling all the laity to form the front lines.[1] Indeed, we are the advance troops in the life of the Church. It is you and I who are rubbing shoulders with all those living and working in the world—in neighborhoods and schools, in the workplace, and in the social sphere.

The Second Vatican Council makes it very clear that the lay faithful have a vital apostolic mission. It's a mission that only

---

1. John Paul II, Apostolic Exhortation on the Vocation and the Mission of the Lay Faithful *Christifideles Laici* (December 30, 1988), no. 9. Vatican website: www.vatican.va.

we can carry out. It's worthwhile reading and reflecting on the words of the Council's admonition to the laity on this matter.

The Council reiterates the call of Our Lord that we be leaven in the world, changing the world from within.

> But the laity, by their very vocation, seek the kingdom of God by engaging in temporal affairs and by ordering them according to the plan of God. They live in the world, that is, in each and in all of the secular professions and occupations. They live in the ordinary circumstances of family and social life, from which the very web of their existence is woven. They are called there by God that by exercising their proper function and led by the spirit of the Gospel they may work for the sanctification of the world from within as a leaven. In this way they may make Christ known to others, especially by the testimony of a life resplendent in faith, hope and charity. Therefore, since they are tightly bound up in all types of temporal affairs it is their special task to order and to throw light upon these affairs in such a way that they may come into being and then continually increase according to Christ to the praise of the Creator and the Redeemer.[2]

The Council Fathers make it clear that every layman is commissioned to the apostolate by Jesus himself.

---

2. Second Vatican Council, Dogmatic Constitution on the Church *Lumen Gentium* (November 21, 1964), no. 31. Vatican website: www.vatican.va.

> The lay apostolate, however, is a participation in the salvific mission of the Church itself. Through their baptism and confirmation all are commissioned to that apostolate by the Lord Himself. Moreover, by the sacraments, especially holy Eucharist, that charity toward God and man which is the soul of the apostolate is communicated and nourished. Now the laity are called in a special way to make the Church present and operative in those places and circumstances where only through them can it become the salt of the earth. Thus every layman, in virtue of the very gifts bestowed upon him, is at the same time a witness and a living instrument of the mission of the Church itself "according to the measure of Christ's bestowal."[3]

Our role is to witness to the life and teaching of Our Lord, Jesus Christ. We are to the world what the soul is to the body.

> Each individual layman must stand before the world as a witness to the resurrection and life of the Lord Jesus and a symbol of the living God. All the laity as a community and each one according to his ability must nourish the world with spiritual fruits. They must diffuse in the world that spirit which animates the poor, the meek, the peace makers—whom the

---

3. *Lumen Gentium*, no. 33.

Lord in the Gospel proclaimed as blessed. In a word, "Christians must be to the world what the soul is to the body."[4]

So, the apostolate is a vital aspect of the Christian vocation. The laity are not second-class citizens in the Church. We are indispensable. If the Church is to grow and thrive, it is the laity who will make that happen. It's our role to bring Jesus and his teaching into the world in a natural and organic manner. We can't perform this role, however, without the necessary preparation. As it is said, we can't give what we don't have.

---

4. *Lumen Gentium*, no. 38.

Striving for Holiness

Our destiny is unity with God, our Father, for all eternity. That is, we are all called to be saints. We are called to be holy. Jesus made this clear when he said, "You, therefore, must be perfect, as your heavenly Father is perfect" (Mt 5:48). Of course, we will be spending our entire life struggling to achieve this goal. But we have to believe that it can be done. Jesus wouldn't call us to do something that we can't do.

What does our struggle for holiness have to do with our mandate to be apostles? St. Josemaría Escrivá said, "Your apostolate must be the overflow of your life 'within.'"[5] Quite simply, if we are not struggling to grow closer to God through a life of prayer and frequent access to the sacraments, we won't have the spiritual wherewithal to be effective apostles. We can't urge others to pursue a life of holiness if we are not struggling toward holiness ourselves. And we shouldn't think that mere

---

5. Josemaría Escrivá, *The Way* (Princeton: Scepter, 2001), no. 961.

activity, even reaching out to others with the message of the gospel, will win us our place in heaven. Jesus said,

> Not every one who says to me, 'Lord, Lord,' shall enter the kingdom of heaven, but he who does the will of my Father who is in heaven. On that day many will say to me, 'Lord, Lord, did we not prophesy in your name, and cast out demons in your name, and do many mighty works in your name?' And then will I declare to them, "I never knew you; depart from me, you evildoers." (Mt 7:21–23)

So, what does this struggle for holiness look like in practical terms? Apostles have a plan of life that brings them closer to Our Lord despite their defects and failings. Apostles frequent the Holy Mass and the sacrament of confession; they spend time each day in mental prayer, praying the Rosary, and reading the New Testament and a spiritual book. Receiving regular spiritual guidance is also crucial. All the while they are striving to grow in the virtues and cast off their vices and defects.

The idea, of course, is to enkindle the fire of our love for God and our fellow man. With the love of God blazing within us, we'll be well disposed to bring others closer to the one who has changed our lives so fundamentally.

Growth in Our Knowledge of the Faith

We can't love someone we don't know. So, it's important that we make our religious formation a priority. We need to study the Faith through regular spiritual reading and reading Scripture. Of course, taking advantage of other forms of religious instruction offered by our parish, nearby universities, or other organizations, as well as the various online venues can be very helpful in expanding our knowledge of the Faith. Nevertheless, just fifteen minutes or so a day of reading from the New Testament and a good spiritual book over time will enable us to acquire a good knowledge of the Faith. It's very important to get some good advice from a knowledgeable person on the best books to read. Good spiritual reading will not only improve our knowledge of the Faith; it will also provide us with material on which to reflect and bring to our prayer. An advisor can guide our selection of books to enable us to acquire good doctrinal knowledge and ascetical formation.

I know this sounds like a lot—and it is a lot. But, if we use our time well and avoid wasting time on such things as television, surfing the internet, and social media, we can have a demanding spiritual plan of life as well as an active and fulfilling family, professional, and social life.

First Prayer and Mortification— Then Action

The most important part of our apostolate is prayer and mortification for our intentions. Our Lord provided us with many examples. Before all of the "important" moments in the public life of Jesus, he prayed. He prayed on the mountainside all night before choosing the twelve apostles. He prayed to the Father before raising Lazarus from the dead. He prayed in the Garden of Gethsemane at the beginning of his passion. And then, of course, he prayed as he suffered and died on the cross. Ever aligned with the will of Our Lord, St. Josemaría Escrivá said, "First, prayer, then, atonement; in the third place, very much 'in the third place,' action."[6] Before getting together with a friend or colleague, even if we have no plans to initiate a conversation that may touch upon matters of faith or morals, we should pray for that person and even offer

---

6. Escrivá, *The Way*, no. 82.

some mortification (prayer of the senses) for him or her. We might not put cream in our coffee that morning, for example. We have to keep in mind that the apostolate is primarily the work of the Holy Spirit. We are the paint brushes in the hands of the Master. Though he doesn't need us to do his work as the artist needs his brushes, the Holy Spirit wants us to cooperate with him. We are an integral part of his plan of salvation.

Our guardian angels and the guardian angels of our friends can be effective allies in our apostolic undertakings. When we have a friend that we are trying to help, we should get all the assistance we can. Ask our friend's guardian angel to join us in prayer and ask for the grace we and our friend need at this time. This is a supernatural undertaking. We would be foolish not to round up all the supernatural help we can.

We can also ask our friends to pray for the friends we are trying to help. We don't have to identify the friend in need. Simply ask your friends to pray for your special intention. Our Lord knows what our friend is praying for.

Mortification is a very underrated form of prayer and it is very pleasing to God. "Without mortification nothing can be done." These words are attributed to St. Philip Neri. Indeed, Our Lord has called us to carry the cross daily (Lk 9:23). These crosses may or may not be voluntary. Whether it's the traffic jam we have to endure during our morning commute or the cold shower to which we subject ourselves at the start of the day, we can offer these annoyances or discomforts to God specifically for the friends we are trying to bring closer to Our Lord. Our mortifications and self-denial are prayers uttered in the privacy of our hearts. They are prayers that no one else will notice. They may be very small things, like getting out of bed immediately when the alarm goes off or taking a little less of the food we like or a little more of what we don't particularly like. We could delay taking a drink for a minute after taking a run or stand when we'd prefer to sit. We could engage in the "drama of the butter" as St. Josemaría used to say. "Today I took butter; today I didn't take butter."[7] You get the idea.

By resorting to prayer and mortification before we unleash our "unparalleled" powers of persuasion, logic, and reason, we acknowledge that the real work is being done by the Holy Spirit. We need him if we expect to have any success in the apostolate. We're just poor instruments trying to cooperate with God's designs.

---

7. Escrivá, *The Way*, no. 205

The Witness of Everyday Christian Living

A very effective form of apostolate is the everyday witness that devout Catholics provide by living their faith in the middle of the world. Although we don't live our lives as committed Christians for show, other people can't help but see. A virtuous life is evident to the people who live around us. They see how we live the virtue of charity in dealing with others. They see our cheerfulness and our willingness to serve. They can't help but see that many of us have more children than average. We would certainly have more children if we were less concerned about acquiring material things.

When someone in the neighborhood learns that we go to daily Mass and frequent confession after getting to know us and sees that we are filled with joy despite all the struggles associated with raising a big family, they take note. Everyone wants to be happy, and it looks like we've found the answer.

Of course, this doesn't mean that we have the perfect family and live the perfect life. But, on balance, there is a contrast. There is no question that people want what we have. There is meaning and purpose to our lives. We have a lot of friends—good friends whom we care about and who care about us. We are filled with joy and our faith is important to us. People see this. And that's a good thing.

It's worthwhile to consider that we witness to Christianity by the way we live our lives. In particular, we should consider when our witness is less than exemplary. We are all sinners. We all drop the ball from time to time. Let's think about our witness when we lean on the horn of our car if another driver is too slow or when we show our impatience with a cashier who is not processing a transaction as quickly as we would like. These lapses happen to all of us. But let's strive to make them exceptions rather than the rule. We need to remind ourselves that we are Christians and we're called to a higher standard.

Although our witness speaks loudly, much more loudly than any words we can bring to bear in an apostolic encounter, our apostolate must be more than living an exemplary Christian life. Our Christian example is, indeed, crucial and without it our words become hollow. Still, we are all called to evangelize the people around us by sharing the Good News with them verbally. We can't be afraid to talk to our friends and listen to them. We need to explain to them what makes us "tick." They want to know. They need to know!

Apostolate in the Family Setting

St. Josemaría Escrivá taught that "Christian couples should be aware that they are called to sanctity themselves and to sanctify others, that they are called to be apostles and that their first apostolate is in the home."[8] How does a married person evangelize in the home? First and foremost, married people evangelize their children through their good example. Mothers and fathers provide their children with their most important models of holiness. Children see their parents struggling to live the virtues. They also see how they live their plan of life—sacraments, prayer, reading, the Rosary, and so forth. Our one-on-one conversations with our children about aspects of the Faith should supplement the children's more formal religious education in school or the parish religious education program.

---

8. Josemaría Escrivá, *Conversations with St. Josemaría Escrivá*, (New York: Scepter, 2007), no. 91.

It's very important that parents avoid developing a critical spirit. I'm not suggesting we put our heads in the sand and fail to acknowledge the many problems in society and in the Church. But we shouldn't dwell on them. A steady drumbeat of criticism of the Church or Father So-and-So can poison children's view of the Church. Our kids need to see that despite the human defects in Holy Mother Church, we love her deeply. The parents' cheerfulness and affection for each other and the children combined with their obvious love of Our Lord and his Church will, more often than not, attract the children to the Faith.

Apostolate with one's spouse is a little trickier. A husband should strive to be a wonderful husband and father, putting his wife first and being attentive to her needs. Of course, the same principle is true for the wife. In striving to be an exemplary Christian, one's spouse can't help but notice how their faith influences the rest of their life. They will see how you struggle to overcome your defects and will appreciate your efforts. One can recommend a date night where you attend a lecture or other formative religious event at the parish or elsewhere. You might combine this with dinner at your favorite restaurant. And, of course, we need to pray and offer mortifications for our spouse. It would also be important to let our spouse know that we are willing cover for them at home watching the kids if they would like to attend a recollection or a weekend retreat.

Another approach that can be helpful is fostering a friendship with another couple who you know are faithful, serious Catholics. In addition to all the wonderful things that come with friendship, the husband of this couple may take an apostolic interest in your husband and help to bring him along in growing closer to Our Lord. Conversely, the husband may seek a couple whose wife may be able to evangelize his wife. This can be very helpful to our kids as well, as they develop friendships with the children of families whose parents are on the same page as you and your spouse. It's important that our kids see other families that take their Catholic faith seriously and are struggling to grow closer to Our Lord. Imagine the impact if the dad of your child's friend reinforces what you are doing by, for example, bringing your child along with him to make a visit to the Blessed Sacrament some Saturday afternoon. That's the kind of conspiracy we want to encourage.

Extended Family

Apostolate with the extended family is not so tricky and we can be much more direct. As with all apostolic endeavors, the motive is love and the well-being of the person involved. We need to meet them where they are in their faith journey and try to be sensitive and understanding without ignoring the truth. This can be very challenging regarding some moral issues. The important thing is that we care about the others and that we look for opportunities to help them with both material and spiritual matters.

We shouldn't be afraid to bring up a topic that might be sensitive, like an irregular marriage, cohabitation, or missing

Sunday Mass. Obviously, these issues should be approached with tact and sensitivity, and always one-on-one and in confidence. We should be prepared for pushback and we should respect their desires if they don't want to discuss the matter. But, don't fall for the "it's none of your business" argument. We love this person. They are part of our family and eternity is at stake. It may be uncomfortable. But it is your business! If they don't want to calmly discuss the issue or simply disagree, keep in mind that you've planted a seed. It may take years for the seed to germinate, but the planted seed, watered with your continued prayers and mortification, may eventually yield the fruit you seek.

Many of your extended family will know that you are a faithful Catholic and will seek you out when questions arise. This will be facilitated by your cheerfulness and your demonstrated concern for them. You can take the initiative by fostering a friendship with your extended family members at family gatherings and one-on-one get-togethers from time to time.

Another approach, particularly if family members live far away, is to email good articles or podcasts that may help them in their spiritual life or that address other matters of faith and morals. It would be good to feel them out as to whether the emails are welcome. It wouldn't help to irritate them with unwanted spam emails. Even someone who is somewhat lukewarm toward the Faith may find them interesting. And, of course, you never know when you've planted a seed that may

FAMILY-RELATED APOSTOLIC STORIES

PAUL'S STORY:
"I Urged my Grandmother to Regularize her Marriage"

My paternal grandmother married my grandfather sometime in the 1920s. She was Catholic and he was Episcopalian. In those days so-called "mixed marriages" were especially frowned upon. My grandmother experienced so much grief for wanting to marry a non-Catholic that she left the Church and raised their only child, my father, Episcopalian. I don't believe they were terribly devout. They were nominally Episcopalian.

About twenty-one years later my non-Catholic father married my Catholic mother. They had six children and my father eventually converted to the Catholic faith.

Sometime after I was married and had several children myself, I wrote my grandmother a letter urging her to return to Catholicism. We lived on opposite sides of the country, so we didn't see each other often. She never answered my letter. And she never brought it up when I called her. So I began to pray for her through the intercession of St. Josemaría Escrivá.

One evening a few years later I received a phone call from my grandmother. She called to tell me that she and my grandfather were getting married in the Church that evening. My grandfather was also received into the Church. They were about eighty-five years old. They both died a few years later.

A couple years ago I was at a family reunion. My five brothers and sisters try to get together once a year. It turns out my brother had a tape recording, given to him by my deceased mother, of my grandparents reciting their wedding vows. I found myself dabbing my tears. What a moment!

ISABELLE'S STORY:
"Praying for My Children's Future Spouses Has Yielded Abundant Fruit"

When my children were adolescents, I read a book that said I should be praying even then for their future spouses—that they be brought up in a faithful and loving atmosphere by parents whose own marriage was committed and intact. I started then and there to pray every day, but in my own way, for "the future spouses of my children . . . that they may all be good Catholics who love you and love your mother, Lord."

The years went by and boyfriends and girlfriends came and went, most of them non-Catholic. My children stopped going to Mass on Sundays even though they attended Catholic universities or had ready access to the Newman Center on campus. One daughter became engaged to an alcoholic who was not practicing the Christian faith (thank God, she ended the engagement . . .). Worst of all, another daughter had a disastrous marriage (to a non-Catholic), which ended in divorce less than a year after the wedding. She had not been married in the Catholic Church.

I started to question my prayer. Was I doing the right thing, praying for the future spouses to be Catholics? My own husband isn't Catholic and yet he's a wonderful man who raised our children in the Faith, sent them to Catholic schools, and continues to accompany and support me on my path in the Church. After talking to friends and then a priest, I decided yes. The prayer is a good one. The sacrament of matrimony is a blessing of grace that is given each day.

My prayers were answered! Two of our three children just recently married. The one with the disastrous first marriage? Her new husband is Catholic and they married in a church devoted to Our Lady. The Memorare is one of my daughter's favorite prayers now. I am overjoyed to see so many blessings abound in her life.

Our son married a beautiful young woman in a non-Catholic ceremony with a special dispensation from the Church. But a few weeks before the wedding, I invited his fiancée to do a Rosary pilgrimage with me on May 12, Our Lady's month and also the feast day of Bl. Álvaro del Portillo (whose beatification I had attended). She had never prayed the Rosary before but was so sincere and loving in saying the prayers that it took my breath away. That evening at dinner with our son, she announced that she wanted to enter the Catholic Church. I almost fell off my chair! She begins Rite of Christian Initiation of Adults (RCIA) in the fall and will be a member of the Church before their first wedding anniversary.

I'm still praying for the third to meet her future spouse and for my husband to enter the Church. God and Our Lady know just when and where that will happen. I trust their judgment! I've learned to never give up on praying in this specific way. After all, if I am a committed Catholic, it's because I know that I enjoy the fullness of the Faith. I want that for my husband and our growing family, too.

LILLIAN'S STORY:
"Prayer and Continued Non-Judgmental Friendship Helped My Troubled Sister Return to the Church"

God works in mysterious ways and in his own timing. Hard times can bring us closer to God when we realize we need divine help and pray.

My sister went through some very difficult times during her troubled marriage and divorce, as it had always been her greatest desire to have a holy marriage and many children. In her despair, she looked for acceptance away from the Church, which led her deeper into a life of misery. I wanted to help her, but besides prayer I wasn't sure what else to do. Sometimes I shared religious ideas and books. I wasn't sure how she would react, but thankfully God heard my prayers and brought her home.

She shared that in her times of greatest anguish there was one gift that God provided. She told me that my continual prayers and genuine love were her saving grace. She shared with me that my spiritual guidance without condemnation helped her return to the Church and the sacraments, for which she is eternally grateful.

Upon my sister's return to the Church, God then blessed us both by allowing us to become pilgrims traveling together to Fatima, Italy, and the Holy Land, and it was my sister who brought up the idea and paid for the trips. The fruits of the pilgrimages continue to enrich our prayer lives, and we shared some of our experiences of the Holy Land through writing a Scriptural Rosary book. Without my sister's struggles and return to the Faith, there wouldn't have been these blessings that we both received. The biggest blessing, of course, is that she is now a devout Catholic.

JONAH'S STORY:
"Friendship and Conversation Helped a Cousin Resume Practicing the Faith"

I met my cousin Mike at a family wedding about ten years ago. We quickly became friends. I discovered that we were seventh cousins through some genealogical research a family member had done.

I walked into his office one day and noticed there was a small statue of Buddha on his desk. I asked him about it, and he said he was a Buddhist but not practicing. I was very surprised because, as I told him, most of our family are Catholic, going back hundreds of years. He said that, many years earlier, he had dated a Korean lady who introduced him to Buddhism. He liked the fact that "they didn't have sin." He asked me if the Catholic Church had gotten rid of sin yet. I looked at him and said, "Seriously, Mike?"

Mike said he fell away from the Catholic Church many years before, when he was a teenager attending a boarding school. Mike said he was "sexually harassed" by one of the brothers who taught there and was turned off from the Church because of this. I told Mike, as I told my kids during the more recent scandals, not to base your faith in Jesus Christ on the failings of human beings.

He eventually married and started attending services at a Protestant church (Methodist I believe) with their daughters. They eventually drifted away from church services after their daughters went off to college. None of them are practicing Catholics today.

About a year ago, Mike was stricken with a serious and rare illness that required surgery that only a few doctors had performed. His wife and daughters were out of town at the time, so I met him at the hospital. We had a talk about whether he was prepared to meet the Lord, to which he responded, "Probably not." At that point I offered to find a priest to come visit with him. He agreed and thanked me.

I contacted a priest I knew, and he agreed to visit with him. Soon after, my priest friend heard Mike's confession, gave him Holy Communion, and agreed to give him spiritual direction. My wife began to send daily reflections, and I started forwarding Bishop Barron's Daily Gospel Reflections.

Mike began attending Sunday Mass a few weeks later, after rehab from his surgery. I went with him the second Sunday he was back in his church, and he has been attending Sunday Mass for over a year now. He is trying to get his wife and daughters back into the Church. My wife and I will work with him on this project.

JOSEPH'S STORY:
"We Helped a Troubled Young Family Member Blossom into a Happy Young Woman of Faith"

A number of years ago my cousin was divorced. She had three children and life at home was pretty chaotic. Her sixteen-year-old daughter, Grace, was having significant problems and was vulnerable to making some seriously bad decisions. My wife and I offered to have Grace live with us, a few hours' drive from her family. She jumped at the chance to move away from home, not knowing the rules she would have to live by as a member of our large family.

Soon after she arrived at our home, my wife told Grace that she needed to go on a spiritual retreat. After objecting strenuously, she finally relented and made her first retreat.

We also enrolled Grace in a nearby Catholic all-girls high school about which she was not particularly thrilled. Nevertheless, she attended the school for three years and graduated.

It was amazing to watch how Grace blossomed gradually over time. She slowly developed into a wonderful young lady of faith. She went off to college and was one of the few students who attended daily Mass. She made many friends and evangelized them.

It is clear that Grace just needed the right environment in which to thrive. We were able to give her a stable family setting. Her school and the friends she made there provided her with a healthy and supportive community. And she discovered the richness of the Catholic faith. Grace has now graduated from college; she has a good job and is living with her father. We love getting together with her from time to time, and my wife and I continue to think of her as a daughter.

NOELLE'S STORY:
"I Offered to Give My Niece and Nephew Religious Instruction"

I recently realized one of my nephews had not received his First Communion. He is going into fourth grade. Due to the pandemic and his parents' reluctance to stay on track with the Faith, things had gotten away from them. There is, thankfully, no animosity toward the Faith and they do seem to want this for their children, but they have focused on other priorities during the past few years. I offered to try to spend some time with him to talk about matters of the Faith and help to instruct him. And, happily, they have asked me to also include one of his sisters who is going into second grade. This family lives several hours away so it will be a challenge in terms of how and when I can meet with the children, but I hope to be able to do this on some of my visits there.

Apostolate in the Parish

The parish may seem like an unlikely place for apostolate. By definition the people there are "connected" to the Church. Many are attending Holy Mass every week and receiving Communion. Probably fewer, however, are going to confession regularly, and even fewer have any semblance of a plan of daily spiritual practices involving daily Mass, mental prayer, Scripture, spiritual reading, or Holy Rosary. Unfortunately, many married couples likely use artificial contraception. The level of understanding of Catholic doctrine for many is probably fairly rudimentary. Many Catholics stop studying the Faith when they graduate from eighth grade or high school. And a significant percentage of the parishioners believe that a woman should have a "right" to have an abortion. This, unfortunately, is the sad truth. Maybe your parish is different. But this is an apt description of many parishes. So, our parish can, indeed, provide fertile ground for evangelization.

While we acknowledge that this may be the situation in many parishes, we certainly don't feel any sense of superiority. We can all say, "There, but for the grace of God, go I!" We are in a position to evangelize only because we have been evangelized ourselves at some time in our lives. We've been blessed profoundly, and now we just seek to be effective instruments in God's hands despite our own sins, defects, and weaknesses.

Apostolate in the parish, as with all apostolate, is based on friendship. We need to get to know the people in the parish and foster genuine friendships. In order to do this, we have to interact with them enough to form the basis of friendship. The parish activities are nearly all run by volunteers—so, we should try to volunteer to help out in the various programs run by the parish. We can teach in the religious education program, serve as ushers, help count money, help with pre-Cana programs, or join the social outreach committee. These are great ways to serve our parish and meet our fellow parishioners. If we make the effort, we can get to know some of them well and form lasting friendships.

If you have children in the parish school, you can get involved in the Parent Teacher Association or other school activities. This is a great way to get to know other parents in the school. And you can be sure these parents will be quite a diverse group. Some will be devout Catholics and others may not know what the inside of the church looks like. We need to be open to everyone we meet. If we make the effort, we will hit it off with some and become good friends.

We shouldn't be shy about initiating new programs or activities at the parish. If there isn't an active men's group or women's group, why not start one? This would be a great way to meet people in the parish. This is especially important for the men of the parish. Women tend to be natural networkers and to have an easier time making friends. Men need male friends, and a parish men's group could fill an important need.

Book discussion groups can also be a wonderful way to make new friends. And the discussions can lead to much deeper relationships. As a parish activity, the club could focus on books that have religious themes, but it could cover other kinds of books as well. The important thing is to provide an opportunity for meaningful discussion.

Another possibility would be to start a marriage mentoring group. You'd probably want the pastor or another parish priest to be involved in this. With his help, older couples who have successful marriages and good Catholic formation could be asked to be mentors to younger married couples. This could provide an excellent service to the parish and lead to some deep and lasting friendships.

It's also a good idea for parents to get to know the parents of their kids' friends. Invite them to your house for a cookout or something simpler like a cup of coffee. As you get to know them, you'll learn more about their values and what's going on in their homes. You'll certainly want to have a good handle on this before you allow your kids to play at their friends' homes or have sleepovers. This practice can also result in friendships that last throughout your child's years at the school and beyond.

PARISH-RELATED APOSTOLIC STORIES

ROB'S STORY:
"My Comment Helped a Young Man Avoid Making a Big Mistake"

There was a parishioner whose son was planning to go away for the weekend with his girlfriend. As this greatly concerned my friend, he wanted me to talk with his son at some stage. I told my friend that I had a lot of work to be done at my house such as painting and various repairs. If his son was interested, we could work on some of these projects together and get to know each other. I had found that working shoulder to shoulder with other men is a great way to bond and develop a deeper friendship. He liked the idea. So the three of us met and had a beer together.

As we chatted, I conveyed a little anecdote about how I courted my wife, in particular how I stayed at my friend's house in his basement during our courtship and that my fiancée and I both rented another house that she could stay in. I explained that we did this so we could more easily live chastely. Even though it cost quite a bit more, it was worthwhile in preparing for marriage properly. I was able to slip these points in between jokes and other lighthearted conversation. Thankfully, this approach worked well, as the next day he decided not to go on that weekend with his girlfriend but instead to go somewhere else with his other friends.

VERONICA'S STORY:
"I Helped a Boy Learn to Pray the Hail Mary"

There was a boy in my seventh-grade parish religion education program class whom I'll always remember. He came to class each week wearing a hoodie, with his head and half of his face covered and his hands tucked deeply into the pockets. He didn't want to take it off when I asked, so I didn't bother pushing it. I was teaching all the mysteries of the Rosary to the class over several weeks and noticed he wasn't learning any of them. He came up to me one day after class and said he just couldn't do it and really didn't even know how to pray the Rosary. We had gone over that in class, but it was still hard for him to understand. He had such a sincere and almost anguished look in his eyes, so I showed him a YouTube video on how to pray the Rosary and told him just to focus on learning the Hail Mary. About two weeks later, he stayed after class and slowly, but proudly and lovingly, recited the Hail Mary. I do believe that was the holiest Hail Mary I have ever heard. I will remember him always, and I'm sure Mary holds him dearly in her heart.

MARIE'S STORY:

"Preparing Second-Graders for First Communion Brought Me Closer to God and Enabled Me to Evangelize Their Parents"

Few things can move you closer to the Gospels and to Christ than having to teach about them. For that reason, an old friend in our parish, Linda, gave me a true gift and acted as a great apostle four years ago when she convinced me to become her assistant teacher, catechizing second-graders who were preparing for their First Communion.

I don't know if I ever read the Bible so closely, or made sure to understand Catholic teachings so well, as when I was preparing to teach class. Soon I became a head teacher, and had the opportunity to instill in these children a knowledge of their faith and a love of the Eucharist.

There's more, though. Our director of religious education was very intentional about roping in the students' parents. She knew that we had an opportunity to not only catechize the children but also to evangelize their parents. First Communion could be a mere formality or an opportunity for nice pictures and a big party, but we tried to make it a re-conversion moment for parents.

I don't know what our batting average was on this goal of bringing parents more fully into the fold, but I do have some measures. Here's one: At least five parents of the students I taught subsequently became catechism teachers. In fact, when my family and I left that parish due to our relocation, my replacement to teach the next year's second-graders was a dad whose son I had taught.

Those five parents are now being catechized by being catechists, just as I had been.

Apostolate in the Workplace

The suggestion that we should be apostles at work likely will lead to some raised eyebrows. Just how do you do that and keep your job? Clearly, our interactions with our coworkers need to be discreet and respectful of the range of religious beliefs held by them. Before we even begin to think about apostolic initiatives at work, we need to look inward and consider what kind of workers we are.

If personal holiness is a prerequisite for effective apostolate, we need to focus first and foremost on sanctifying our work and sanctifying ourselves in our work. How is that done?

Sanctifying our work begins when the alarm clock goes off in the morning by getting out of bed without delay and offering our work and our entire day to God. We continue our day, using our time well and weaving our plan of life into our day from morning until evening—including Mass, mental prayer, the Rosary, and gospel and spiritual reading. Of course, maintaining a demanding plan of life in the midst of pursuing excellence at the workplace and the demands of family life requires us to use our time very well. We should always be on the lookout for ways we waste time and try to make the needed adjustments. A spiritual advisor can help us to ramp up our plan of life gradually over a period of time and in a manner that takes into consideration our personal circumstances.

We sanctify our work by offering it to God and doing it very well. As a result, we should have a reputation as an outstanding employee, someone who can be relied upon to get the job done at a high level. We sanctify our work by struggling to live the virtues in the workplace. We live the virtue of order by keeping our desk or work area neat. We don't procrastinate. A good habit is to try to do the most disagreeable task first, offering it up for one of our intentions. Seeking holiness in the workplace also means living the virtues of justice and patience and having a spirit of service.

Sooner or later our coworkers will learn that we are Catholic and many will find out that we are serious about our faith. This will come out during our conversations at lunch or the chitchat that takes place just prior to a meeting getting started. Maybe on a business trip your colleagues will learn that you like to attend daily Mass early in the morning before business meetings begin. This knowledge will frequently lead to conversations about religion and possibly some moral issues. The respect that your colleagues have for you as a highly competent and valued worker will make you that much more credible when you speak to them about religious or moral issues. I remember years ago there was a woman in the office who had a reputation for being a slacker. One day I stopped by her cubicle for some reason and noticed a Bible on the corner of her desk. I cringed. Of course, I was happy to know she was a Christian and apparently read the Bible. But I was dismayed by the fact that many coworkers would associate her Christianity with her being negligent in her work.

As with all apostolate, friendship is the foundation of the apostolate in the workplace. You can try to cultivate friendships with your coworkers by suggesting they go out to lunch with you from time to time. Your lunchtime conversations will likely cover the whole spectrum of topics ranging from sports to politics to work issues to family activities. It's also likely that religion and moral issues will come up in conversation. Knowing that you're a serious Catholic, your colleagues may seek you out to discuss some of the religious or moral issues on their minds. We need to take advantage of these occasions. Our conversations should be tactful and discreet. But we should never hold back on the truth, even if we expect some opposition. Speaking the truth at that time may be just what your friend needs to ponder how they are living and any changes that need to be made.

As your friendship deepens, you can take the initiative and bring up matters that may or may not be welcome. If you know that your colleague is cohabitating with a girlfriend or boyfriend, you would be doing a favor by pointing out the problem with that situation. With your friendship as the basis for your concern, your friend will likely understand this and not take offense. They may not change right away, but you've planted the seed!

If you are in the habit of going to Mass at noontime, you might try inviting a Catholic colleague to accompany you. He may decline. But then again, your invitation may be the beginning of deeper devotion to the Eucharist for your colleague. At some point you might share some aspects of your plan of life with your colleague and suggest that they consider taking some time for mental prayer each day, or maybe for praying the Rosary. As you get to know your colleague better, you'll know the right time to bring up these personal matters related to developing a deeper interior life.

When you've established a good friendship at work, you can suggest some good books, articles, or podcasts that may help your colleague in their spiritual life or better grasp some moral issue. They may even be ready to accompany you on a weekend retreat.

As we previously discussed, apostolic initiatives must be accompanied by a lot of prayer and mortification. Prior to getting together with a friend or colleague it's good to bring your meeting to your prayer, asking for light in dealing with your friend and the grace to be an effective instrument of the Holy Spirit.

WORKPLACE-RELATED APOSTOLIC STORIES

NICK'S STORY:
"Sharing Interests Led to Friendship and Conversion"

A number of years ago my law firm hired a lawyer named Bill. He was a huge baseball fan, so I started following his team, since he loved to talk about it. From time to time, we would watch games together, and he would explain the intricacies of baseball strategy to me. Bill's background was nominally Lutheran, though he had not been brought up as a practicing Christian. Knowing I was a devout Catholic, he would sometimes ask me questions about faith and morals. He was a good guy, and found the Catholic teachings he heard fascinating. He was very attracted to the meaning that Christ's death and resurrection gave to life, and he thought the Church's teachings about human sexuality, while difficult, were very beautiful.

There's a lot of downtime in baseball games, which gave us plenty of time to talk, and after a while, we were spending more time talking about the Faith than about baseball. After a couple seasons, he decided he wanted to become a Catholic, and he was received into the Church the next Easter. He married a wonderful Catholic girl, and now they have a big, happy family.

JACOB'S STORY:
"Sacred Art and Beauty Led to Conversion"

The archbishop of Florence asked me to found the Sacred Art School of Florence in 2011. Before doing so, I befriended a young American teacher from another art school there who shared a common interest in sacred sculpture. He had almost no religious formation of any kind. He met another American there and they eventually got married civilly. During our conversations we talked about the importance of marriage. Since we were both sculptors, he could relate to my work and its sacred aspect. Interestingly, sacred art helped him recognize the Faith and the importance of it.

Later, he and his wife asked if they could convert to Catholicism. So I prepared them for a year through catechesis. We worked through the *Catechism of the Catholic Church* from front to back every Wednesday after dinner at my house. This would also lead to some great conversations about the Faith.

It turns out this young man's father was very anti-Catholic. In fact, some time before, when my friend was visiting Rome, his father threatened that if his son converted to Catholicism, he'd disown him. When the time came for my friend and his wife to receive the Sacraments of initiation, his father came to Florence because he was wondering what was going on with his son. He attended the Holy Thursday ceremonies in the Duomo and he sat in front of me. The cardinal archbishop was about ten feet away and when he saw that the cardinal washed the feet of the people, his preconceptions of Catholicism vanished, and I saw him start to cry. I could see his body vibrate as he sobbed. I realized then that there was a tremendous grace occurring. After Holy Thursday

Mass, as we were leaving the cathedral, he turned around to me and said, "What do I need to do to become Catholic?" So I said, "Well, if you want you can attend catechesis for a year. Come to my house every Wednesday and we'll have dinner and study the Catholic Faith."

So that young couple was baptized in the Duomo that Easter. They were also confirmed, received their First Communion, and renewed their wedding vows—all in one night.

DAMIAN'S STORY:

"A Colleague Returns to the Sacraments After Being Away Since Childhood"

My office hired a new intern named Henry and I was assigned to take him under my wing, show him around, and train him. Over the span of a few months, Henry and I got to know each other, and the more we spent time together the more he started opening up about his personal life and his career goals. I regularly attended noontime Mass at a church close to the office. One day I mentioned to Henry that I was going to Mass, at which point he shared that he had been baptized in the Catholic Church but had fallen away from both the Church and the Faith because of his family life. The oldest of three children, at a young age he had been compelled to take care of his two younger siblings so that his mother could work after his father abandoned them. He shared that his family used to go to Sunday Mass, but that over time his mother stopped taking the children to Mass altogether. I invited him to go with me to Mass, but he politely declined.

A short time later, while working on a project, Henry casually asked me why I went to Mass every day. This question started us on a long and ongoing conversation covering a wide range of topics including what the Mass is, why going to Mass is important, sin, and man's need for a savior. A few weeks later, Henry mentioned to me that he was thinking of going to Mass, but that he had not received the sacrament of reconciliation since his first confession. I immediately suggested to him that we go to Confession that day just before Mass. Henry agreed. We arrived at the church a little early and I handed Henry a pamphlet on how to make a good confession. We entered the church, did an examination of conscience, and got in the confession line. Henry made his second confession ever, attended Mass with me, and started going to Sunday Mass.

ANDREW'S STORY:
"I Suggested a Colleague Come With Me to Confession"

A number of years ago I was working in downtown Washington, DC. I tried to attend Mass at noon on days when I couldn't attend in the morning at my local parish. One day I happened to be chatting with a colleague and mentioned that I was planning to go to Mass at noon and go to confession before Mass. He was intrigued and mentioned that he hadn't been to confession in many years. The next day he asked if he could come along with me to confession and Mass. On the way back to the office he thanked me and said he felt like a new man.

KRISTEN'S STORY:
"Daily Mass and Faith Discussions Helped a Coworker See that Abortion is Wrong"

On a business trip, four of us shared a rental car to get from the airport to our hotel. I have the devotion of going to Mass each day, so my first task after arriving in a new city is to look up Mass times in the nearest Catholic Church as well as the number of a taxi. I jotted these down inside my notebook. In our first meeting, a coworker noticed my notations. He conferred with the others and then came to offer me the use of the rental car. They all wanted to ensure that I could get to Mass each day. Since they didn't know any young professionals who went to daily Mass, they began asking me questions about the Faith.

Over time, one of these coworkers, Mike, brought up moral topics at lunch with me that he and his wife found challenging. In particular, they thought that a woman should be free to have an abortion if she wished. Mike and his wife were both raised Catholic but were no longer practicing the Faith. I prayed for them and asked God for the right words to say to this good man. One day, Mike shared the great news that they were expecting a baby. I was volunteering at a pregnancy help center at the time and knew a lot about fetal development, so he asked a lot of questions. One day he came into my office and closed the door behind him and looked very intense. I knew something important was on his mind. He said, "My wife and I are now pro-life, and I wanted you to know that we understand that all life is precious and abortion is wrong."

CECELIA'S STORY:
"Inviting a Colleague on a Pilgrimage and Retreat Deepened Her Prayer Life"

After becoming friends with a woman at work, I invited her to accompany me on a May pilgrimage to a nearby shrine dedicated to Our Lady. After the pilgrimage we had several conversations about the Faith and the importance of fostering a life of prayer. Eventually, I invited her to attend a retreat, which was the first time she had been invited to one since she moved to the US from overseas. She attended with me and had a fantastic retreat and has been trying to be more consistent in her prayer life.

ADAM'S STORY:

"My Student Came to the Truth of the Church While Seeking the Truth in Reading Great Thinkers"

Through my enthusiasm as a teacher, I encountered a graduate student at my university who was equally passionate about liberal education. During a conversation at the cappuccino bar on campus about the revival of classical education in charter schools around the country and the variety of approaches to liberal education at the university level, we decided to team up and teach a course on the history of liberal education. The student came from a secular background with respect to both his family and his education in public schools and university. Together, over the course of a semester we read the classic texts on liberal education—Josef Pieper's *Leisure the Basis of Culture*, Evan Brann's *Education in the Republic*, Christopher Dawson's *Crisis of Western Education*, John Senior, Leo Strauss, Louise Cowan, Frederick Wilhelmsen, and others. We had different approaches but were equally excited about understanding the history of university education in the nineteenth and twentieth centuries. We never explicitly discussed faith in Jesus Christ or the claims of the Catholic Church to be Christ's one, true Church, but the authors' witness as truth-seekers spoke to him as a truth-seeker himself and he came to encounter Jesus Christ as the Logos, through whom everything was made and holds together. He had not been baptized as a child, so it was a blessed day when he received all three sacraments of initiation—baptism, confirmation, and Eucharist.

EVAN'S STORY:
"I Helped an Employee and Friend Get Married in the Church and Avoid Committing a Serious Sin"

When I was managing an investment firm, there was a young man whom I had hired as a financial advisor trainee. He was a terrific young man with a solid Catholic family background. As was typical in those days, my wife helped me to really get to know the folks that were working for me. We did a lot of socializing with people in the office. Consequently, we both got to know this young man's fiancée. They were both practicing Catholics, so I was astounded when one day in the office he asked me if he could have a week off so that the two of them could go to Europe for a honeymoon with only the benefit of a civil marriage. "Why aren't you having a Nuptial Mass?" I asked. He replied, "We just found this fantastic last-minute bargain airfare and hotel, which requires us to leave four days from now. We'll have a civil ceremony before we leave, and a Nuptial Mass sometime later." Undeterred by political correctness, I responded that they were committing grave sins, and asked if they would give me a chance to solve their problem if I could. He laughed nervously and said that would be fine, but doubted that I could get their six-month waiting period waived, their Pre-Cana instructions arranged, and a church reserved all in three days. I quickly contacted a priest friend of mine and asked him if he could help. To make a long story short, the waiver was secured, my priest friend gave them an intense round of classes, and my wife and I, along with his parents, attended their very intimate Nuptial Mass in a Catholic church three days after that initial conversation. That couple and

MATT'S STORY:
"I Believe I Helped My Protestant Boss Grow Closer to Our Lord"

I had a boss who also became a friend; we were peers in age and in some experiences. He was a nationally recognized leader in his field. In faith he was a mainline Protestant who rarely attended church. He and most of our office team were Midwestern practical idealists, liberal but cost-conscious, and pro-choice. The work environment was totally secular; faith was never mentioned.

As we became friends, I felt a growing desire to share the Faith with him. I invited him to meet a priest friend. My boss agreed and went to the meeting, which began a series of occasional meetings over the years with this priest and another priest with whom I was friends. My boss also joined me in daily Mass when we traveled, and he attended a three-day retreat. He particularly enjoyed praying the Rosary in a group.

My boss has not yet become Catholic. However, he was strengthened, given hope, and brought closer to God.

WILL'S STORY:
"Guiding a Business Partner's Father Into the Church"

I started a business in Chicago with a partner who was not Catholic and really practiced no faith. I tried hard, through many conversations and prayers, to lead my partner closer to God, but to no avail. However, I got to know his father and through casual conversation learned the father had gained an appreciation for the Catholic Church through the services his son with Down syndrome had received at a Catholic home for the disabled. Those conversations led to the father eventually converting to the Catholic faith. During the process he was diagnosed with terminal cancer. I completed his RCIA at his hospital bedside, and prior to his being called home to heaven, he was received into the Church.

DOUG'S STORY:
"Correcting a Colleague's Tardiness to Mass Led to a Lasting Friendship"

Probably forty-five years ago I had a coworker who was always sarcastic and giving me a rough time. I did notice, however, that when I attended daily Mass at a church near our office he would always arrive late, just in time to receive Communion. (It was about a ten-minute walk from the office.) He was never hesitant to give me a hard time about even the smallest things, so one day I commented to him, "What's with the corner cutting on God, coming late to Mass?" After that, he would come on time and offer a prayer of thanksgiving afterward. He's been consistent over the years since and has become a personal friend.[9]

GREG'S STORY:
"A Real Estate Transaction Led to Friendship and Marriage After Years of Living Together"

The beginnings of this relationship were certainly not auspicious. As I am in real estate, it is common to receive letters in the mail asking me to consider selling a particular property I own. I received such a letter from a gentleman about a property I did not plan to sell. But the gentleman followed up with a personal note, and then a phone call.

While I still did not plan to sell the property, I respected his persistence and his polite respect. We had a couple of conversations in which I shared my experiences in real estate.

It was months since our last correspondence, and I was in the process of retiring and selling most of my real estate. So, when he offered the fair market value (usually such folks want a hugely discounted price), and said if we sold it without a realtor I could save over $15,000, I decided to sell.

Selling without a realtor means all the back-and-forth goes directly between the buyer and seller. I found this much better

---

9. Normally, I would recommend giving such a fraternal correction with tact and sensitivity. Obviously, these individuals had a certain rapport that allowed them to communicate in a rough-and-tumble manner. God's grace prevailed in this instance.

than working through the middleman of a realtor, and we got to know each other fairly well.

At the time he had been living with his girlfriend for years, with no intentions of getting married. They were both atheists. But our houses were only blocks apart, and we continued to keep in touch, talk real estate, and discuss his new purchase.

As we got to know them, we could see that the woman wanted to marry very much. And eventually my wife and I were able to bring up the topic and gently but persistently urge them to get married soon. Within a year of our friendship, they were wed, with us attending.

At first, children were out of the question. They both had good jobs and didn't want anything to interfere with their careers. But as they got to know our family, they were attracted by the joy and harmony of our large family (we have nine children). Within a year of being married, their first child was on the way. Now, with their first child only eight months old, they are discussing how they could have another child.

As to the Faith, there is growing interest. Most recently, the wife asked for separate meetings with me and my wife. She said what has struck her is the kindness and peace of our grown children, and she wants to know "the secret." In private talks with the husband, he has said he now believes in a "guiding spirit" who has things "under control."

ASHLEY'S STORY:

"Conversations with a Student Revived Memories of Her Grandmother's Life of Prayer"

Meetings over coffee with one of my students enabled her to ask the questions that were in her heart about her faith. In our conversations, she would talk about her family, particularly about her grandmother and how it was her grandmother's prayer life and example that etched into her memory images of what a life of faith was all about. When my student started coming to a class on Catholic doctrine I taught, those memories triggered something in her, and brought her back to the Faith. Our coffee conversations sealed the deal, so to speak, as my student explained to me how she saw God's hand rescuing her throughout her life. Our one-on-one conversations were where our friendship and trust developed and really helped her discover friendship with God.

MICHAEL'S STORY:

"Simply Being a Faithful Practicing Catholic Helped My Friend Return to the Sacraments"

I had a very good friend in college with whom I had much in common. We both sang in the school choir throughout our college years and had an interest in the ancient philosophers like Aristotle, Plato, and Cicero. My friend was raised Catholic but had drifted from the Faith. Throughout our college years we had numerous deep conversations, many of them philosophical and many at least pointed to various truths of the Faith. We tried to get together over dinner once a week to have our discussions. Of course, he knew that I was a practicing Catholic and frequented the sacraments. It wasn't obvious to me what kind of impact our friendship and my religious faith was having on him, until I received a letter from him telling me that I was the reason he had returned to receiving the sacraments. We continue to be great friends.

Apostolate in the Social Sphere

We interact with our friends, neighbors, and others on a regular basis. We can use these social interactions to deepen our friendships and establish new ones. Through these friendships we can bring some souls closer to God. As in other settings, expanding our friendships in the social sphere can require a certain amount of initiative. A good start is just being friendly. I go for a fifty-minute walk just about every day in my neighborhood. I try to make a point of greeting everyone I encounter on my walk: other walkers, bikers, and those walking their dogs. It amazes me how few people would even make eye contact with me if I didn't greet them with a "Good morning" or a "How ya doing?" Most people respond with a smile and an appropriate response. Yet, without my greeting, no words would be uttered. Granted, my greetings so far have not led to any lasting friendships. But who knows, someday they might. Nevertheless, being cheerful and approachable can't help but facilitate meeting people in a social setting.

There are many ways of getting to know the neighbors better. I have a neighbor who is very outgoing and has organized neighborhood block parties. Our street has an adjacent cul-de-sac, and we would set up our grills, tables, and chairs there. All the neighbors would be invited, so inevitably I'd meet someone I didn't know very well. The block party would give everyone a chance to catch up and get better acquainted.

Another neighbor has recently organized a monthly lunch for a small group of the retired men in the neighborhood. It's a pretty diverse group. Some are Catholic and some are not. It's been a great way to deepen friendships and get to know others better.

Cocktail parties can be a good way to meet new people and catch up with old friends. I'm often reluctant to go to cocktail parties, but I usually wind up enjoying myself when I go. It's a good practice to try to focus on meeting and getting to know at least one person at a party. We can do this by asking the people we meet about themselves. Dale Carnegie, in his classic book *How to Win Friends and Influence People*, said, "You can make more friends in two months by becoming interested in other people than you can in two years by trying to get other people interested in you."[10] If you feel you've "hit it off" with someone at a party, go ahead and exchange contact information and arrange for lunch or coffee within the next couple weeks.

The prospect of attending a large conference, fundraiser, or meeting can be daunting. Typically, there are many people

---

10. Dale Carnegie, *How to Win Friends and Influence People*, updated (Simon & Schuster: New York, 2022), p. 81.

there we don't know. The introvert in us tells us that for that very reason this is not the kind of event we'd like to attend. But, for the apostle these kinds of events can present a great opportunity. Even if we are not inclined to attend, we should seriously consider going, if for no other reason than the prospect of meeting new people and expanding our circle of friends. In other words, an apostolic incentive should move us to "bite the bullet," take a risk, and attend the event. The worst-case scenario is that we attend as a mortification for one of our intentions and we meet no one of interest. The best-case scenario is we offer our attendance as a mortification and then meet one or more very interesting people.

SOCIAL-RELATED APOSTOLIC STORIES

JAMES' STORY:
"I Helped a Friend Live Holy Purity"

A decent but not yet close friend from college days moved into town, and we started to socialize more steadily than in college. One day, I picked him up at his apartment and there was a *Sports Illustrated* swimsuit issue on the floor. I spoke up, basically a moment later, to say that's not good for a Christian man and how we need to keep our hearts pure. He said thank you, but I couldn't tell if it was sincere or not. Years later, then married and a faithful Catholic, he made a point of thanking me, saying the shame of that moment of fraternal correction (and our continued friendship) prompted an enormous change in his life, causing him to take his spiritual health and purity much more seriously. I was surprised, as we'd never talked about that moment again. I'm godfather to his son now.

ERIN'S STORY:
"I Formed a Catholic Catechism Club for Neighborhood Girls"

Back in 2010 a military family moved into the house across the street. There were three girls in the family, ages seven, ten, and thirteen. After getting to know their mother, I realized that the girls, who were in public schools, were not enrolled in the parish religious education program. Neither was a girl who lived in the house behind me. All four of these girls were Catholic, seemingly without any formal religious instruction and immersed in a post-Christian public school system.

Somehow, I figured out that something should be done to assist their religious formation. Knowing that their lives were surrounded with sports and cultural activities, I perceived that the idea of a catechism class had been missing. I engaged two of my nearby Catholic friends who had daughters within the same age range as my neighbors, and they enrolled their daughters in my new class. With their help, we persuaded the neighbor girls to join as well.

Rather than sugarcoat the club with a fun name, I just called it Catholic Catechism Club. We met at my home twice a month and we went through the old Baltimore Catechism. Since it was on a weekday after their school day, we had a quick snack first and then a Q & A on the catechism. The girls, for the most part, paid close attention and seemed to be interested and, as a bonus, I was able to make close friends with my neighbors. The club lasted for three years before situations changed and the young ladies moved on.

Twelve years later, we still stay in touch, though the family across the street moved to Texas several years ago and the girls have mostly graduated from high school and a few from college.

LAURIE'S STORY:
"Friendship With an Elderly Neighbor Led to Her Returning to the Church"

Helen was in her early eighties when my husband and I moved in next door to her with a six-month-old baby girl. Helen was hard of hearing, found it difficult to walk, and had a thousand stories to tell. In the course of the next six and a half years we grew to be dear friends. She had raised five daughters and worked in the public schools as a cook. She always had a great smile and was eager to welcome each of our new babies (every sixteen months or so). She and her husband became a third set of grandparents for our children. People would sometimes remark how kind I was to spend time with the elderly neighbor. In fact, she was my dear friend. In the evenings, when the kids could be grouchy because it wasn't dinner time yet, she'd sit with me on the back patio swing. She'd tell me funny stories and gush over how adorable my children were as they clamored about on their bikes and on our swing. In the lowest parts of my days, she would help me to love my children more.

Helen loved cream in her coffee. Whenever I splurged and bought half-and-half, I'd give her a call and say, "I have cream!" She knew it meant good coffee and she'd come over and we'd sit for a cup. She knew that I had many things to do, but a cup of coffee with cream and a good friend was a needed break. During one of our coffees, she lamented that she and her sister were the last living members of her large family. Her sister had severe dementia and Helen was suffering and feeling very alone. She wondered what God had in mind by all of this. For my morning prayer that day, I had read the "wrong" reading in the spiritual book, *In Conversation with God*.[11] Each chapter has reflections on the readings of the day's Mass. It was Tuesday but I had read Wednesday's reflection, all part of God's plan for my day. The reflection I read was "God's Suffering Children." It addressed why God allows suffering for his dear children. I gave it to her. I explained that I found it helpful and she only needed to read two pages of this little book. She took it. The next morning, she knocked on my door and said that she finished the book last night and wanted to know if I had more for her to read!

Over time, I learned that she was raised in a large Catholic family, that her husband was not Catholic, and that she tried to raise her five daughters in the Faith. Over time, she drifted away

11. Francis Fernandez, *In Conversation with God: Meditations for Each Day of the Year (7 Volume Set)* (New York: Scepter Publishers, 1993).

from the Faith as did all of her children. With this great book, *In Conversation with God*, she wanted to come back to her faith but was nervous about the "next steps." One day over coffee I mentioned that our parish was having a penance service with inspiring speakers and an opportunity for confession. Because of her poor hearing, I was basically yelling at her about how much God loves her and wants her close to him! I handed her the flyer. I thought I was doing a pretty convincing job of explaining (yelling) the value of confession, but she was only catching bits and pieces. God made it clear to me that he was giving her the grace (I was not the compelling one) when she said, "Do you know what, they even have confession during this, so I could go to confession!"

I drove her; she went to confession and came out beaming! Helen began coming to Mass on Sundays with our squirmy family. Her husband saw the change in his dear wife and thought it was better that he take her to Mass rather than "impose" on us every Sunday. So they both became regulars at Mass. Her husband passed away about a year later. As far as I know, he didn't convert to the Catholic faith, but on his deathbed the main concern that he expressed to his beloved wife was, "Who will take you to Mass when I'm gone?" She reassured him that we would.

MARILYN'S STORY:
"I Helped a Classmate Avoid a Huge Mistake That Could Have Ruined Her Coach's Life"

During my overnight senior high school trip from Philadelphia to New York City, my teachers placed me in the same hotel room as two classmates. Diane, the granddaughter of a Holocaust survivor, was on her way to an Ivy League university with a full scholarship to play squash. Mary struggled with anorexia and had a tongue piercing; she and I often disagreed when class debates touched on women's rights. After we had turned off the lights, Diane asked for advice about her squash coach, for whom she had developed a strong crush. He was married with a baby. Mary chimed in right away: "Oh, you're probably in such better shape than his wife, you can totally get him," and continued with some advice on seducing young men. That gave me a few moments to think before I asked, "So, what do you see in this coach?" Inevitably, her attraction had a lot to do with his dedication to his family and faithfulness to the sport. From there, Diane could see that the qualities she loved about her coach would be jeopardized by seducing him away from his wife and child.

Fast forward to that fall, when we were all back at our public high school for homecoming weekend. Diane literally climbed over some tables and chairs to tell me, "At college, whenever I'm not sure what to do, I ask myself, 'What would you do?'"

BENJAMIN'S STORY:
"My Love for Mary Led a Girlfriend Back to the Sacraments"

While at university I sang in the school choir. There I met a girl who was a fallen-away Catholic and we became good friends. At one point the choir made a trip to Portugal. I knew that while in Portugal I wanted to go to Fatima and I convinced the group, which was largely Protestant, to go. When we arrived at Fatima the leader of the group asked me to give a talk on Fatima and its history, since I was the one intent on going and knew the most about it. So I delivered my talk on the fly and we all toured the Shrine of Fatima, which for me was an incredible pilgrimage.

My friendship with the girl I met at choir deepened quite a bit and eventually we started dating. While we were dating, we hung out frequently with my Catholic friends, until finally my girlfriend said we had to stop dating so she could figure things out. We stayed in touch but did not see each other much. At one point I wrote her a letter, which she failed to answer. Finally, she wrote me a letter in which she thanked me for introducing her to the Blessed Virgin Mary, and that she was now practicing the Faith. She is now married to a good Catholic man and has a few children.

ALEXANDER'S STORY:
"My Love for the Mass Led to a Neighbor Regularizing His Marriage"

One day I was chatting with a neighbor. We had met for lunch downtown during the week. As I recall, it was a fairly wide-ranging conversation. At some point I mentioned that I attended daily Mass and how important it was to me. He listened but didn't really react one way or the other.

A couple months later, we got together again. To my surprise, he mentioned that our previous conversation had got him thinking. It turns out, he was Catholic but was not married in the Church. When he and his wife were in the Peace Corps, they were married in Africa, where a tribal chief officiated the wedding. He wanted to regularize his marriage and get married in the Church. I introduced him to a priest who gave him and his wife Pre-Cana instruction and performed the ceremony. My wife and I were the witnesses.

GEORGIA'S STORY:
"My Prayer Helped Save a Friend's Life and Taught Me About My Vocation"

Jack and I had been friends since fifth grade and in fact he took me on my first official date to the eighth-grade dance, when all the hairspray from my bangs ended up on his dress shirt after just one slow dance. By senior year of high school, our friendship had cooled a lot, especially after he "ruined" my fifteenth birthday party by getting pretty aggressive with one of my best friends, an effect of the anabolic steroids he had been taking to bulk himself up for football.

During that senior year, I made my first five-day silent retreat over Christmas break, as part of my trying to take seriously a vocational call to apostolic celibacy in Opus Dei that I had repeatedly sensed over a two-year stint of intense prayer. The main theme of my retreat was my doubts about the value of following a vocation in the Church and especially about a call to celibacy (because I thought I had a better plan for my life). A few days into the retreat, I perceived a very specific divine inspiration to pray for one of the boys in my American Studies class who was about to die. I even told a friend on the retreat so that she could also pray. I stayed on my knees a lot of the remainder of the retreat, but when I returned to school everyone was still alive and well. "It must have been my imagination," I concluded.

Our final project for American Studies was a presentation, during which Jack confessed to having gotten drunk twenty-five times during the month of December and having driven his car on twenty-one of those occasions, "wanting something bad to happen." This was Jack's response to his father having been diagnosed with cancer. Jack's presentation was a thank you to our teachers for having gotten him professional help and facilitating better communication with his parents, and also to his friends for having alerted the teachers. He didn't know to, or need to, thank me. In retrospect, I know that God saved Jack's life that Christmas. And I learned an important lesson for my own journey as an apostle, namely that the immensity of the value of my vocation includes my getting to witness God save souls around me, that my prayer would facilitate others playing their part even when I was not the protagonist in helping someone, and that the first person God would draw closer to himself through my apostolate would always be me. God answered all my doubts on that retreat.

BRYAN'S STORY:
"Prayer and Friendship Helped a Man Overcome Gender Confusion and Return to the Faith"

One of my college friends, I'll call him Tom, was very helpful in my return to the sacraments when I was in my early twenties. After college, we kept up our friendship, though we were in different cities. Later, Tom went to law school in DC, where I lived, and so we saw each other more often in those years. He came to my wedding, and he is the godfather to my first son.

In the mid-'90s, he emailed to tell me he was now an atheist. It was quite a shock because while in college, he had considered a religious vocation. After discussing atheism over email for a while, he also told me he was a homosexual. I kept praying for him, and we emailed each other fairly often. One Easter, a few years later, he told me he was coming back to the Church, though it was a major struggle for him. I stepped up my prayer. He did return to the sacraments for a while.

Then the real shocker: a few years later, he told me he was identifying as a woman and was changing his name. This stunned me. Our friendship cooled considerably. I didn't know what to say. I just poured on the prayers for him, especially at Holy Mass. A few years went by. No contact. Then, out of the blue, he emailed, saying he realized that he was, in fact, a man, and was now going to the sacraments regularly! I was obviously very grateful for this change. During the COVID lockdowns, we talked over the phone, and he's now living with his elderly parents and helping them. We don't talk all that often, but I think the worst is behind him and he sounds like the friend I had in college—smart, devout, with a great sense of humor. I'm certainly glad he got through these difficult years and landed on his feet, so to speak. After this, I never doubt the immense value of praying for friends, especially at Mass. It's all about the long game.

SAM'S STORY:
"Through Friendship I Helped a Fellow Student See That Premarital Sex Is Wrong"

My friend John lived next door to me in the dorms at my university. We became friends playing soccer and working out together. He grew up without any kind of faith, and being scientifically inclined, chose to make sense of reality through a nihilistic view that infinite variations of the events in life were transpiring simultaneously across a multiverse, and that when our life ends, our existence is simply extinguished. This left him floundering during our walks on campus when I would ask him existential questions among the ivy and the arches: Why do you think we're here? What is the purpose of life? Does God exist? Why should we treat others well? He was deeply dissatisfied with his inability to even begin to answer these questions, and while he was distrustful of religion, he knew with certainty that I was his friend, that for some reason I had a cheerful attitude toward life, that I was religious and not crazy, that I could lift more weight than him, and that I wasn't trying to beat him in an argument.

One day he admitted to me that he was sleeping with a girl he was dating. Under his worldview he figured it was consensual, he wasn't hurting anyone, and it didn't matter anyway; but Our Lord in his mercy provoked his conscience and gave him a feeling that he might be wrong about some of this. Without appealing explicitly to Catholic doctrine, I asked him to think beyond the pleasure of sex to what must be its deeper purpose and proper context. I helped him to see that there is purpose and order in the world; that it stands to reason that an act that is ordered to the creation of children should only be played out in a context where parents bound to each other in marriage could be open to raising children in a stable manner; and that anything short of that would be using the other person, which is undignified and harmful in many ways. To his credit, out of his open-mindedness, intellectual honesty, and friendship, he ended the relationship with the young lady.

EMMA'S STORY:
"Going to Confession Regularly Moved My Friends to Return to the Sacrament"

In friendship everything comes up eventually, and most of my friends (I think) know that I go to confession once a week. Almost everyone expresses surprise or incredulity when they discover this. Confession, we all think, is the hard sell. I don't even try to sell it, but my friends know it's important to me. In the last few months, I've learned that two friends of mine—who felt distant from the institutional Church and who were shocked when they learned that I go *every single week*—have started going to confession *every single week*! They don't know each other, don't live in the same state, and they didn't tell me this. It just came up casually. The simple mention of it can be powerful.

MEGHAN'S STORY:
"A Chance Encounter With an Older Jewish Woman Led to Her Devotion to the Blessed Mother"

A number of years ago I was living in Miami. One day as I was driving, I saw an older woman fall on the street and break her arm. I drove her to the emergency room to get X-rays. While on the way there I mentioned to her that God works for good through everything in our lives, including misfortunes, though often we don't know how. During the hospital stay to heal her arm, the doctors discovered that she had breast cancer, which wouldn't have been discovered if it wasn't for the X-rays needed to properly set her arm. Cancer treatment was initiated immediately and she recovered fully. This encounter led to a lasting friendship. Though my friend is Jewish, we had many more conversations about religion, and I shared with her aspects of my Catholic faith. Interestingly, she developed a deep devotion to Our Lady. Though I've lost contact with her and she is probably now deceased, I'm certain that her devotion to Our Lady brought her great comfort.

TODD'S STORY:
"A New Friend Felt Comfortable Sharing With Me Because of Our Common Backgrounds"

I met Zach at a retreat. In our first meeting we discovered we had three things in common: we had both attended the same university; we both had the same degree (master's in education); and we both came on retreat at the same retreat center as non-Catholics! Needless to say, we had much to discuss, and we exchanged emails at the end of the retreat.

Zach had many, many questions about the Catholic Faith. Perhaps the fact that I too had been non-Catholic made him more comfortable with being open and honest. In any case, after long letters back and forth, he decided to become Catholic, and asked me to be his sponsor.

In fact, he was getting his RCIA training at the same church where I had received my instruction. He joined Mother Church on the Easter Vigil, the same ceremony at which I had been received into the church thirty-five years before!

DAVID'S STORY:
"My College Roommates Told Me About the Real Presence and I Later Converted to Catholicism"

The apostolic outreach that looms largest in my memory is one for which I was the target. As an eighteen-year-old freshman at a secular university, I thought myself to be a "science alone" atheist. My high school and puberty had long since torn away the superficial low-church Episcopalian beliefs of my childhood. I had been baptized and confirmed in the Episcopal Church and even had served as an acolyte. But no one had ever described the Eucharist as anything other than a symbolic liturgy.

At college I did not attend any church services. Who did? Well, two of my three Catholic suitemates did. Both these guys were already my good friends. I also admired their intelligence. So, when they revealed that they attended Mass on Sundays and I asked one of them why, I expected a serious answer. "Because God is there, Jesus is there," was the response. "You mean as a symbol, right?" I replied. "No, really there, really, in substance, body, everything." I was floored by this totally unexpected answer.

Not long after, I went down to the nearest Catholic church, two blocks away, to see for myself. When I entered, I was struck by a rich floral odor. There was no one else there. I was clueless about tabernacles, so I had no direction to pray toward. I just intensely asked Our Lord if he was there. His clear silent answer was yes. I had an immediate sense of being loved, and relief that the most important issue in life was forever solved.

My other Catholic suitemate gave me Chesterton's *Orthodoxy* right away. I spent the next two years being guided by the university's Catholic chaplain while I worked up the courage to tell my parents. On January 25, 1964, the Feast of the Conversion of St. Paul, I was conditionally baptized and made my first confession and communion.

SARAH'S STORY:
"After Years of Friendship and Prayer, An Illegitimate Marriage is Happily Resolved"

I have a friend whose marriage was not legitimate; therefore, she could not receive the Eucharist. She and her husband were both Catholic; he was married before and had children from his first marriage, and he also had children with my friend. My friend obediently abstained from receiving the Eucharist, and prayed ardently that one day her situation would be resolved and that she would be able to receive Communion in the Church. I told her that her obedience to Church teaching would one day bring about the solution to her marriage situation. We prayed consistently for this intention, cried many times together, prayed Rosaries, and went on pilgrimages for thirty-plus years! Finally, by God's grace and perfect timing, my friend's husband's first marriage was annulled and they were able to get married in the Church. I went to their wedding! It was a testimony of faithfulness, resolve, and steadfast prayer over all these years. The people in attendance (family and close friends) plus the priest celebrant were uplifted by this couple's desire to set straight what was crooked.

The Apostolate of Suffering

We all know people who are suffering to one degree or another. Some may have a serious illness or have a loved one who is very sick. We probably know someone whose close relative has passed away—maybe a spouse or a child. Another may be unemployed for an extended period of time. We've probably also experienced situations when our suffering friends or acquaintances impressed us with the supernatural manner with which they handled their situation. They were cheerful despite their struggle. We could see that they placed their futures and those of their loved ones in God's hands. They helped us feel the presence of God in our lives. Indeed, we were edified by witnessing their Christian approach to suffering.

Obviously, our suffering friends were given a grace to approach their difficult situations with a supernatural outlook. When it's our turn to be the suffering friend, we can try to convert that suffering into great good. Of course, it's not an easy thing to do in the midst of the turmoil that may be going on in our life. But, if we seek the spiritual support we need from a spiritual advisor and our close friends, we can adopt a Christian attitude regarding our troubles and help those around us to see that life is more than the material well-being that so many are seeking.

The Apostolate of Public Opinion

The apostolate of public opinion is about both correcting errors in matters of faith, morals, or cultural issues that we encounter in the public square, and encouraging those who do a good job communicating about those matters to the public. It's pretty clear that confusion about many fundamental things abound in the public square. For example, we see confusion about the nature of marriage and sexuality at the highest levels of society. Many people, even Catholics, have a poor understanding of the Catholic faith. How can they be reached and helped to understand these important matters? We should strive to help them on a one-to-one basis through our friendship when possible. But we can't reach everyone. The apostolate of public opinion deals with reaching a broad cross section of society through the various means of public communication. This is a genuine form of apostolate and as such should be characterized by charity, reason, and understanding.

How do we carry out an effective apostolate of public opinion? One obvious avenue for shaping public opinion is writing letters to the editors of various newspapers and magazines, both online and paper versions. Prudent use of social media can also be an effective way to reach a number of people with our perspective on many hot button moral and cultural issues. We might consider writing a testimonial on the joys of family life despite its challenges or the benefits of Natural Family Planning. Such an article could be an eye opener for many people. Writing short online book reviews can be very helpful to people considering a book purchase. We should not excuse ourselves from this duty because we're not professional writers. If we have good Catholic formation and a high school education, we ought to be able to craft a letter to the editor that can present the case we are trying to make.

Op-ed pieces are another way to lay out the correct Church teaching or argument from natural law that makes our case. Not everyone may be up to producing effective op-ed articles and getting them accepted for publication. But if we have that skill, we should definitely pursue it. Also, many online publications allow readers to make comments on their articles. We can take advantage of these opportunities to provide our perspective on a range of issues. We should be prepared for a lively exchange with other readers. For some, our views may provide a perspective they haven't considered.

Making brief statements at school board meetings supporting school policies that are consistent with natural law and right reason can be a fruitful endeavor. It would be good to coordinate such presentations with other like-minded parents.

Writing or meeting with senators, congressmen, and other elected or politically appointed officials can be worthwhile. Although we may not change any minds in the short term, over time a steady drum beat of communications from constituents voicing the truth of natural law can lead to change.

In all these communications it's important that we strive to enlighten rather than alienate. Being respectful and demonstrating an interest in understanding their point of view can remove barriers and enable us to carry on a dialogue that may help those with whom we are communicating to see our point of view.

Conclusion

As we have seen, the role of the apostle is a demanding one. Then again, Jesus never said following him would be easy—quite the contrary. But those who love don't count the cost. Christians are motivated by love—love for Our Lord and love for our family, friends, colleagues, and neighbors. Indeed, as we grow closer to God and become more united to him, our apostolic impulses will become second nature. It will become quite natural to want to share the treasure we've discovered. We will probably never think of ourselves as "apostolic dynamos." Ultimately, we may not even think of ourselves as apostles. Rather, we're just being ourselves, being good friends to our friends.

Prayer for the New Evangelization[12]

"'Every one who calls upon the name of the Lord will be saved.' But how are men to call upon him in whom they have not believed? And how are they to believe in him of whom they have never heard? And how are they to hear without a preacher? And how can men preach unless they are sent?" –Romans 10:13-15

Heavenly Father,
pour forth your Holy Spirit to inspire me with these words from Holy Scripture.

Stir in my soul the desire to renew my faith
and deepen my relationship with your Son, our Lord Jesus Christ
so that I might truly believe in and live the Good News.

---

12. United States Conference of Catholic Bishops. https://www.usccb.org/prayers/prayer-new-evangelization.

Open my heart to hear the gospel
and grant me the confidence to proclaim the Good News to others.

Pour out your Spirit, so that I might be strengthened to go forth and witness to the gospel in my everyday life through my words and actions.

In moments of hesitation, remind me:
- If not me, then who will proclaim the gospel?
- If not now, then when will the gospel be proclaimed?
- If not the truth of the gospel, then what shall I proclaim?

God, our Father, I pray that, through the Holy Spirit,
I might hear the call of the New Evangelization to deepen my faith,
grow in confidence to proclaim the gospel,
and boldly witness to the saving grace of your Son, Jesus Christ,
who lives and reigns with you in the unity of the Holy Spirit,
one God, for ever and ever.

Amen.